Science for Kids
39 EASY
ENGINEERING EXPERIMENTS

Other Books in the
Science For Kids Series

Science for Kids
39 EASY
ENGINEERING
EXPERIMENTS

Robert W. Wood
Illustrations by Steve Hoeft

TAB BOOKS
Blue Ridge Summit, PA

FIRST EDITION
FIRST PRINTING

© 1992 by **TAB Books**.
TAB Books is a division of McGraw-Hill, Inc.

Library of Congress Cataloging-in-Publication Data

Wood, Robert W., 1933-
  Science for kids : 39 easy engineering experiments / by Robert W.
Wood.
    p.   cm.
  Includes index.
  Summary: Introduces basic ways we use engineering through such
projects as making a wind tunnel, building a truss, and testing the
action of friction under various conditions.
  ISBN 0-8306-1946-1 (h)   ISBN 0-8306-3943-7 (p)
(p)
  1. Engineering–Experiments–Juvenile literature.
[1. Engineering–Experiments. 2. Experiments.] I. Title.
TA149.W66   1991   91-12612
620'.0078–dc20   CIP
                                          AC

Acquisitions Editor: Kimberly Tabor
Book Editor: Nina Barr
Production: Katherine G. Brown
Book Design: Jaclyn J. Boone
Cover photo by Susan Riley, Harrisonburg, VA

Contents

Introduction

The Science for Kids series consists of eight books introducing Astronomy, Chemistry, Meteorology, Geology, Engineering, Plant Biology, Animal Biology, and Geography.

Science is a subject that instantly becomes exciting with even simple discoveries. On any day, and at any time, we can see these mysteries unfold around us.

The series was written to open the door and to invite the curious to enter—to explore, to think, and to wonder. To realize that anyone, absolutely anyone at all, can experiment and learn. To discover that the only thing you really need to study science is an inquiring mind. The rest of the material is all around you. It is there for anyone to see. You have to only look.

Engineering is the art and science that is concerned with putting scientific knowledge to practical uses and to use power and materials the most effective ways that benefit society. An engineer designs and builds structures such as dams, highways, and skyscrapers as well as airplanes, cars, and other forms of transportation that include high speed trains and ships.

Examples of outstanding engineering feats from the past include the Pyramids of Egypt, the Panama Canal, and the San Francisco-Oakland Bay Bridge. These are just a few of the accomplishments that amaze us with the skill, time, and effort spent by their engineers. They designed the projects, selected the proper materials, and calculated the strength of the structure to make sure it would stand up under the worst conditions it might encounter.

In ancient times, things had to be learned mostly by trying over and over again until the project was successful. But today, a person attends school to learn what engineers discovered in the past. Through education, today's engineers can avoid their failures and can build on their accumulated experience to accomplish even more than engineers from an earlier time.

Engineering includes many different fields, and you can consider each one a distinct profession. Often, these fields overlap and an engineer in one field might need to know something about one or more of the other fields. For example, an aeronautical engineer will design the shape and structure of an aircraft, but he will also have to be knowledgeable about the type of engines that can be used and the hydraulic systems to operate the controls.

Hydraulic engineers are concerned with the design of water systems such as aqueducts, and how much water will flow through different sizes of pipes under different pressures.

A mechanical engineer works with the design of machines, the strength of materials, and how to use gears to accomplish work.

Structural engineering deals with the design of large buildings such as skyscrapers. A structural engineer is concerned particularly with the strength of girders, concrete pillars, walls, and other parts of the structure to be sure that the building can withstand the strains that might be put on it.

Civil engineers design and build projects such as canals, tunnels, roads, and bridges. They must know how to get the most use from concrete, iron, and steel as well as how to efficiently move large amounts of earth with heavy equipment.

Through the science of engineering we have increased our comfort, safety, health, and overall life style. Engineers use scientific knowledge to make the best use of energy and materials.

The following experiments will introduce some of the basic ways we use this important science.

Symbols Used in This Book

All of the experiments used in this book can be done safely, but it is recommended that a parent or teacher supervise young children and instruct them on any potential hazards.

The following symbols are used throughout the book for you to use as a guide to what children might be able to do independently, and what they *should not do* without adult supervision. Keep in mind that some children might not be mature enough to do any of the experiments without adult help, and that these symbols should be used as a guide only and do not replace the good judgment of parents or teachers.

Electricity is used in this experiment. Young children should be supervised and older children cautioned about the hazards of electricity.

Materials or tools used in this experiment could be dangerous in young hands. Adult supervision is recommended. Children should be instructed on the care and handling of sharp tools or combustible or toxic materials and how to protect surfaces.

Flame is used in this project and adult supervision is required. Do not wear loose clothing. Tie hair back. When handling candles, wear protective gloves—hot wax can burn. Never leave a flame unattended. Extinguish flame properly. Protect surfaces beneath burning candles.

1

Gravity and Falling Bodies

Place the pillow on the floor. Hold the book in one hand and the paper in the other hand. Both objects should be level. Hold the book over the pillow (Fig. 1-1). Now drop them both at the same time. The book will hit the pillow first. Try the experiment again, but this time, place the paper flat on top of the book (Fig. 1-2). You will see that they both hit the pillow at the same time.

This result means that in the first try, the resistance of the air slowed the falling speed of the paper. But the second time, using gravity alone, you could see that light and heavy objects fall at the same speed.

Fig. 1-1. *Drop the book and the paper from the same height.*

Fig. 1-2. *Place the paper on top of the book.*

2
Paper Helicopter

Materials
- STRIP OF PAPER (ABOUT 2 INCHES WIDE AND 10 INCHES LONG)
- SCOTCH TAPE
- SCISSORS

Fold the paper in half lengthwise (Fig. 2-1). Make about 10 small bends in one end for weight. Fasten these bends in place with scotch tape (Fig. 2-2). At the other end of the strip, carefully cut down the center of the fold about 4 inches, and bend the two strips out to form narrow wings (Fig. 2-3).

Drop the helicopter from above your head, and it will rotate, slowing its descent. The weighted end creates the center of gravity. Air flowing past the wings cause them to rotate, slowing the rate of fall. Helicopters operate on this principle, and it is the reason that they are called rotary-wing aircraft.

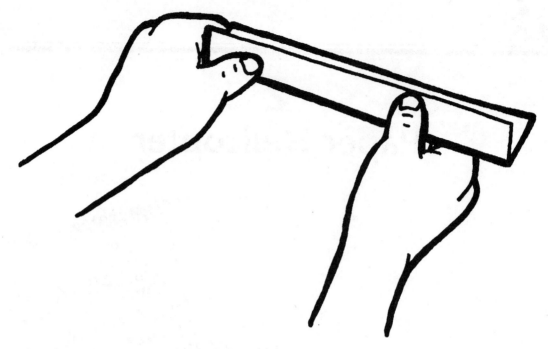

Fig. 2-1. Fold the paper in half.

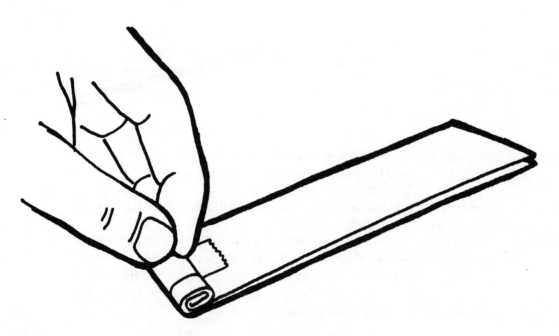

Fig. 2-2. Fasten the bends in place with tape.

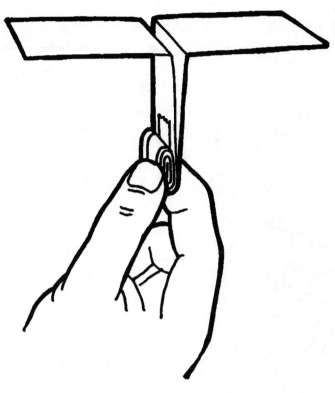

Fig. 2-3. *Fold the strips down for wings.*

3

Reducing Air Pressure with a Funnel

Materials

SMALL FUNNEL

MATCH

CANDLE

With the help of an adult, carefully light the candle (Fig. 3-1) and hold the large opening of the funnel near the flame. Now try to blow out the flame by blowing through the small end of the funnel (Fig. 3-2). The flame will bend toward the open end of the funnel and will be very hard to blow out. If you turn the funnel around and blow through the wide end, you can blow out the candle easily (Fig. 3-3).

When you blew through the small end, the airstream traveled from the narrow part of the funnel to the larger area where it was forced to spread out. This spreading out of the air lowered the air pressure in the opening and caused the surrounding air, which was at a higher pressure, to move toward the open end of the funnel.

Fig. 3-1. *Use a candle to show the flow of air.*

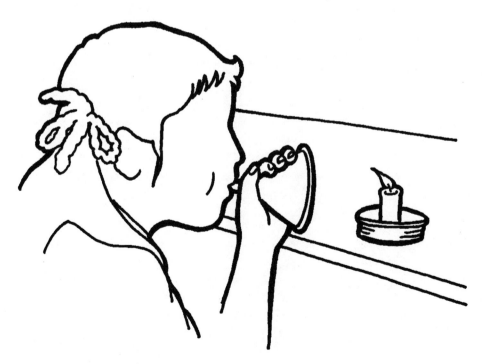

Fig. 3-2. *Blow through the small end of the funnel.*

Fig. 3-3. *Blow through the large end of the funnel.*

4

What Makes an Airfoil

Fold the paper in half so it is about 5 inches long. Hold the ends together, and then slide the top one down slightly so that the paper bends into a narrow loop (Fig. 4-1). Now tape the ends to the cardboard (Fig. 4-2). This makes the bottom of the loop flat with the cardboard and the top half curved. With the help of an adult, plug the fan in and turn it on. Hold the cardboard in the breeze from the fan. Have the taped ends pointing into the wind (Fig. 4-3). The paper airfoil will try to lift from the cardboard. The airfoil is able to lift because air flowing over the curved top is moving fast while the air below hardly is moving. This air flow reduces the air pressure in the area above the curved surface and creates the lifting force. This principle allows the wings to lift an airplane into the air.

Fig. 4-1. *Fold the paper into an airfoil.*

Fig. 4-2. *Tape the airfoil to a piece of cardboard.*

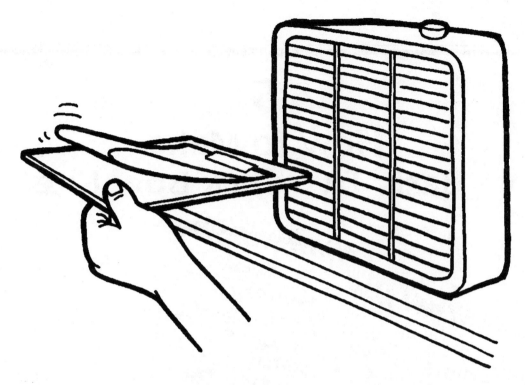

Fig. 4-3. *The breeze from the fan will cause the airfoil to lift.*

5
How to Make
a Basic Two-Stick Bow Kite

Materials
- 2 PINE OR SPRUCE STICKS (1/4 X 3/8 INCH AND 36 INCHES LONG)
- COVERING MATERIAL (PLASTIC FROM LEAF, TRASH OR GARMENT BAG)
- STRING

Materials
- YARD STICK
- SMALL SAW
- SCISSORS
- SCOTCH TAPE OR MASKING TAPE
- PENCIL AND CHALK
- WOOD GLUE

With an adult's help, use the saw to notch the ends of both sticks (Fig. 5-1). Do not cut toward yourself. Measure and mark the center of one of the sticks, and place this point under the other stick 8 inches from one end (Fig. 5-2). Glue the sticks together, and bind the joint with a few wraps of string (Fig. 5-3). Stretch a framing string through the notches in the ends of the sticks to form the outer edge of the kite (Fig. 5-4). Pull the string tight, and tie the ends together with a square knot. Fasten the framing string in place by wrapping a couple of wraps of string around the notch on each side of the framing string (Fig. 5-5). The frame of the kite is now complete.

Place the frame on top of the plastic film to form a pattern. The cross stick should be on the side next to the plastic covering. Use the chalk to mark out the pattern (Fig. 5-6). Mark about an inch outside the framing string on all sides to allow for the flap to fold over the string. Carefully cut out the pattern and fold the flaps over the string. Fasten the flap in place with tape (Fig. 5-7). Now tie a piece of string to the notch in one end of the cross stick. Bow the cross stick until it has about a 4 inch bow, and tie the string in the notch in the other end of the stick (Fig. 5-8). To attach a bridle string, have an adult help you make a small hole where the two sticks cross. Use a piece of string about 5 feet long, and feed one end through the hole. Tie this end around both sticks. Tie the other end of the bridle string through the notch at the bottom of the kite. Tie the string used for flying to the bridle string at a point about 3 feet from the bottom of the kite and about 2 feet from where you connected the bridle string to the cross stick (Fig. 5-9). Shifting this point up or down just a little will adjust the flying angle of the kite. This kite should not require a tail and should fly easily in a light breeze. Always fly your kite in open areas away from power lines.

Fig. 5-1. Notch the ends of the stick.

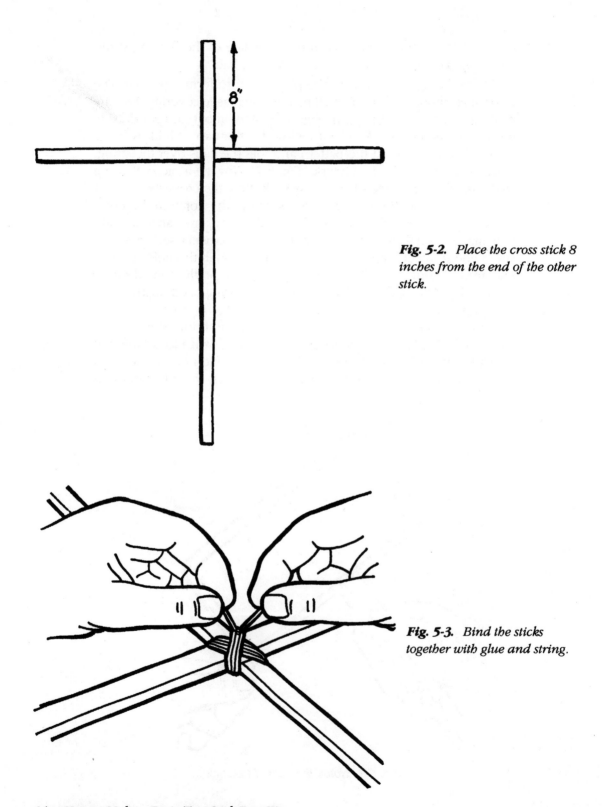

Fig. 5-2. *Place the cross stick 8 inches from the end of the other stick.*

Fig. 5-3. *Bind the sticks together with glue and string.*

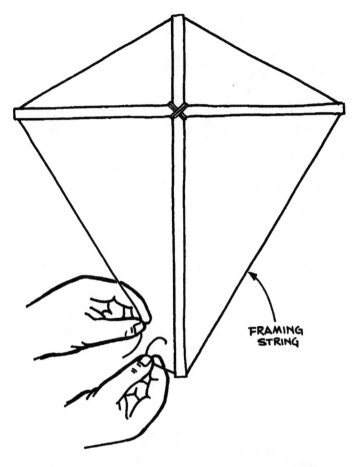

Fig. 5-4. *Attach the framing string to the frame of the kite.*

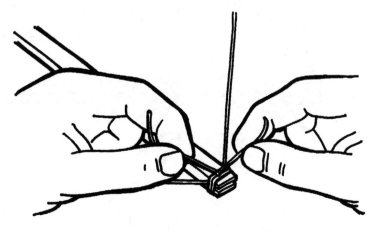

Fig. 5-5. *Hold the framing string in place with a couple of wraps of string.*

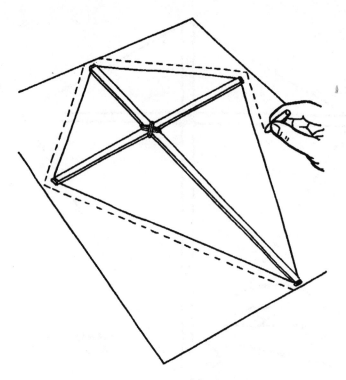

Fig. 5-6. *Mark out the pattern with chalk.*

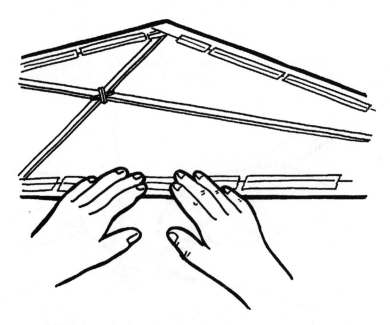

Fig. 5-7. *Fasten the flap in place with tape.*

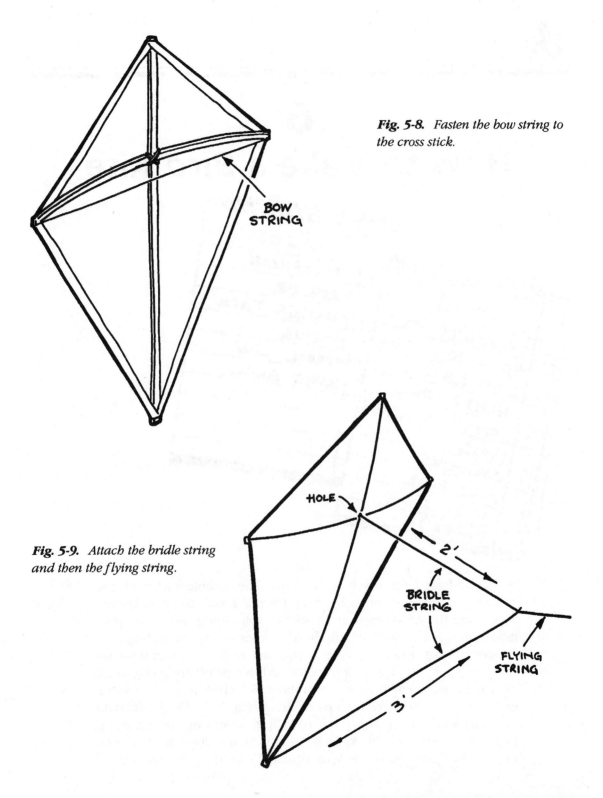

Fig. 5-8. *Fasten the bow string to the cross stick.*

BOW STRING

Fig. 5-9. *Attach the bridle string and then the flying string.*

HOLE

2'

BRIDLE STRING

FLYING STRING

3'

6

How to Make a Bird Kite

Materials

- 1 FLEXIBLE STICK 40 INCHES LONG
- 2 STICKS 26 INCHES LONG
- 1 STICK 10 INCHES LONG
- COVERING MATERIAL (PLASTIC OR PAPER)

Materials

- CELLOPHANE TAPE OR MASKING TAPE
- STRING
- SMALL SAW
- WOOD GLUE

With an adult's help, notch both ends of the flexible stick with the saw for the framing string (Fig. 6-1). Form a V with the two 26-inch sticks, and tie the pointed end together with string. Add a drop of glue to the joint to hold it securely. The other end of the V should be 14 inches apart. Place the 10-inch stick across the V about 9 inches from the open end. Fasten it in place with wraps of string (Fig. 6-2). Now place the 40-inch stick across the V, 5 inches from the pointed end. *Lash* it to the V with wraps of string (Fig. 6-3). Tie the framing string across the V just below the 10-inch stick, leaving enough string to reach the ends of the 40-inch stick. Bow the 40-inch stick back toward the open end of the V to a point 15 inches from the ends of the 10-inch stick. Tie the string here and run it over to the other side. Bow this tip back to match the first wing (15 inches) and tie the framing string through the notch in the bowed 40-inch stick. Next, stretch string across the open end of the V to form an X below the 10-inch stick (Fig. 6-4). Apply the covering material and fasten in place as in the previous experiment (Fig. 6-5). Attach the bridle by using five strings tied from each outer tip of the kite (Fig. 6-6). Tie the strings together about 14 inches from the front of the kite and about one-third of the way from the top. Some adjustment of the bridle might be necessary. You must have a tail of about 20 feet. You can attach the tail to a string running from the two tips at the bottom of the kite.

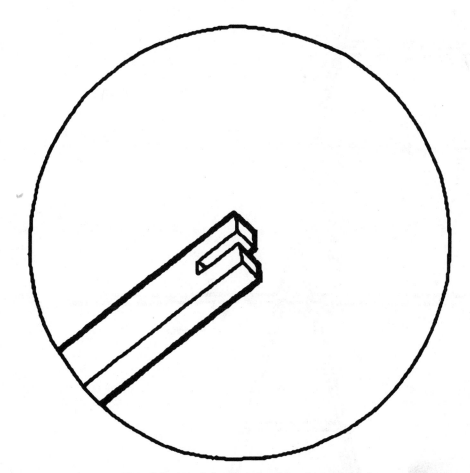

Fig. 6-1. *Notch both ends of the 40-inch stick.*

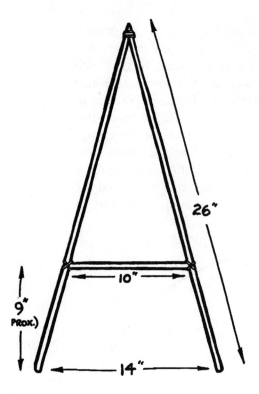

Fig. 6-2. Build a frame as shown from the three remaining sticks.

26"

10"

9" (PROX.)

14"

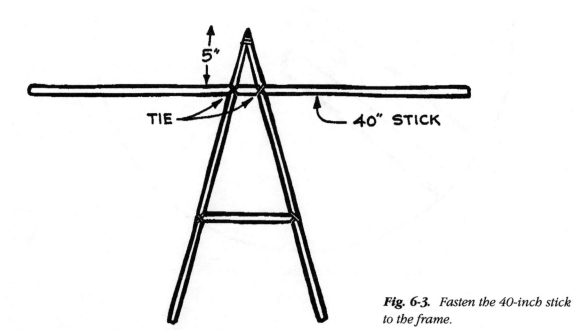

5"

TIE

40" STICK

Fig. 6-3. Fasten the 40-inch stick to the frame.

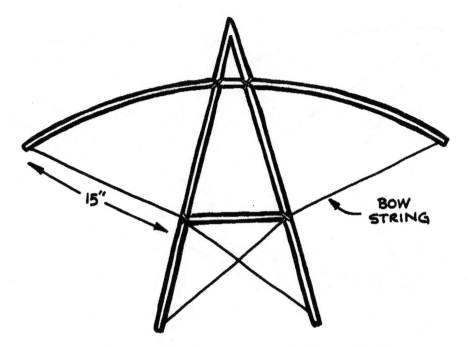

Fig. 6-4. *Attach the framing string to the frame of the kite.*

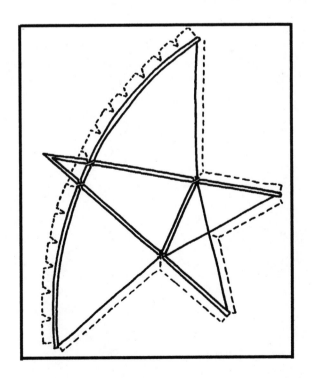

Fig. 6-5. *Mark the pattern on the covering material.*

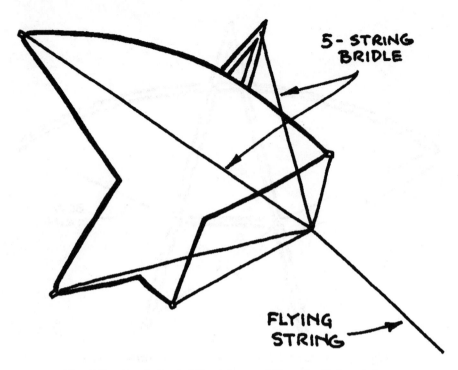

Fig. 6-6. *Attach the bridle string and then the flying string.*

7

How to Make a Wind Tunnel

Materials
- 9 OR MORE EMPTY MILK CARTONS
- TAPE OR GLUE
- ELECTRIC FAN
- KNIFE

With the help of an adult, carefully cut off both ends of each carton (Fig. 7-1) and stack them together in rows of three to form a large open box with dividers. Tape or glue the cartons together. Place an electric fan at one end of the wind tunnel and, with adult help, turn it on (Fig. 7-2). A smooth flow of air will come out the other end. A fan alone produces a twisting flow of air, but the partitions in your wind tunnel help stabilize the flow of air.

To test, hold a lightweight model airplane or piece of cardboard on a string at the end of the tunnel.

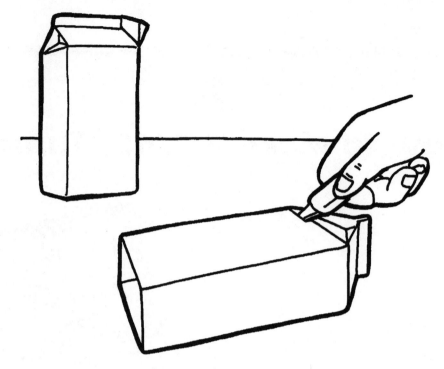

Fig. 7-1. *Carefully cut the ends off the cartons.*

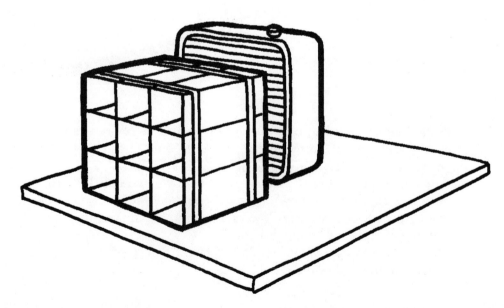

Fig. 7-2. *Fasten the cartons together with tape or glue.*

8

A Paper Airplane for Distance

Materials

- SHEET OF PAPER (8 ½ X 11 INCHES)
- SCOTCH TAPE
- PAPER CLIP

Fold the paper as shown in Figs. 8-1, 8-2, and 8-3, and you will have an airplane designed for distance flight.

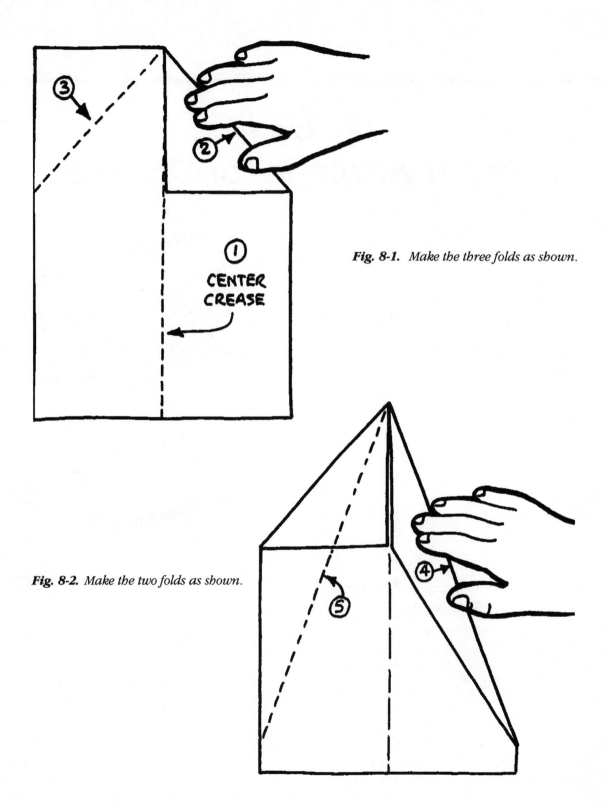

③

② ①

CENTER
CREASE

Fig. 8-1. *Make the three folds as shown.*

Fig. 8-2. *Make the two folds as shown.*

④

⑤

FOLD ON CENTER-LINE:

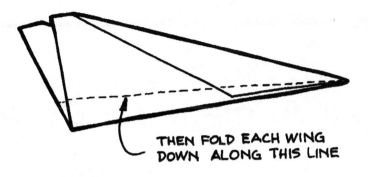

THEN FOLD EACH WING
DOWN ALONG THIS LINE

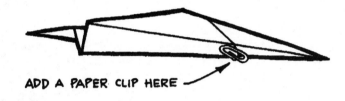

ADD A PAPER CLIP HERE ―

Fig. 8-3. *Fold down the wings and attach a paper clip for balance.*

9

A Paper Airplane for Duration

Materials
- SHEET OF PAPER (8 X 10¼ INCHES)
- SCISSORS

Complete the folds as shown in Figs. 9-1, 9-2, and 9-3 for an airplane designed for duration flying.

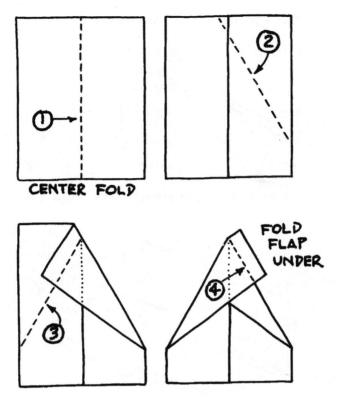

CENTER FOLD

FOLD FLAP UNDER

Fig. 9-1. Make the four folds as shown.

TURN PLANE OVER AND
FOLD BACK THE NOSE...

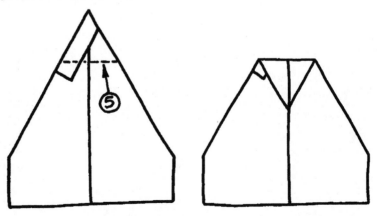

Fig. 9-2. Make the fold for the nose.

FOLD PLANE UP ON CENTER LINE!

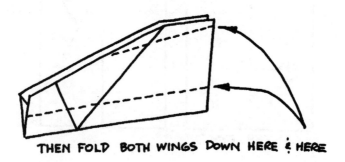

THEN FOLD BOTH WINGS DOWN HERE ¿ HERE

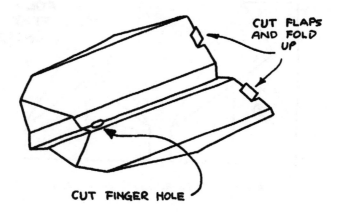

CUT FLAPS AND FOLD UP

CUT FINGER HOLE

Fig. 9-3. *Fold down the wings and make the cuts for the flaps.*

10

A Two-Ring Paper Airplane

Carefully cut two strips of paper about ½ inch wide and 11 inches long (Fig. 10-1). Make each strip into a ring, and use tape to hold the ends together (Fig. 10-2). Tape one of the rings to the side of the straw about two inches from one end. This side will be the front. Tape the other ring to the same side of the straw about one inch from the other end (Fig. 10-3). Launch the airplane into the air (Fig. 10-4). You can change the flight path by moving the rings to different positions on the straw.

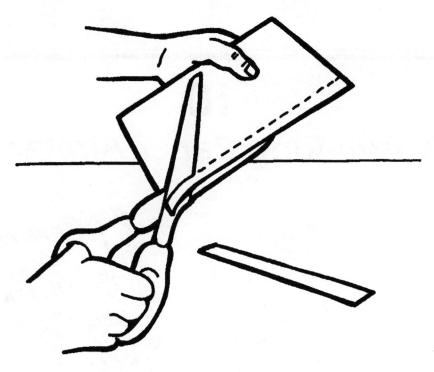

Fig. 10-1. *Cut off two strips of paper.*

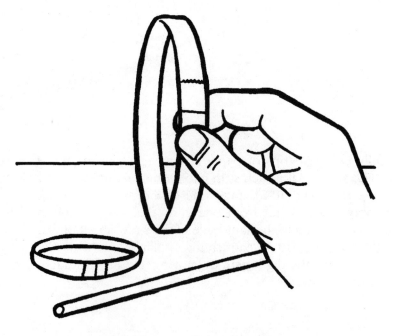

Fig. 10-2. *Form the strips into rings.*

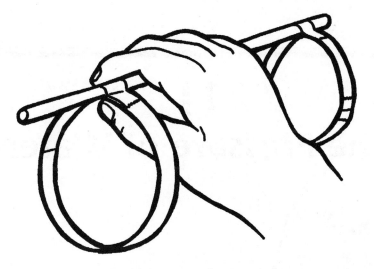

Fig. 10-3. *Fasten the rings to the straw.*

Fig. 10-4. *You can change the flight path by repositioning the rings.*

11

The Pressure of Water

Materials
- MILK CARTON
- CELLOPHANE TAPE
- NAIL
- WATER
- KITCHEN SINK

Have an adult help you punch three holes in the side of an empty milk carton with the nail. Punch one near the bottom, one about the middle, and one near the top (Fig. 11-1). Cover the holes with one long strip of tape (Fig. 11-2). Now fill the carton with water all the way to the top (Fig. 11-3). Place the carton near the edge of the sink with the holes pointing toward the drain, and remove the tape (Fig. 11-4). The stream of water from the top hole will not spurt out very far. The water from the lower hole will spurt a little farther, and the water from the bottom hole will travel the farthest. Water pressure depends on the depth of the water. The stream from each hole has the pressure of the amount of water above that hole. This concept is why some cities have their water supply in raised tanks. It provides water pressure for the water system.

Fig. 11-1. *Make three holes in the carton.*

Fig. 11-2. *Cover the holes with tape.*

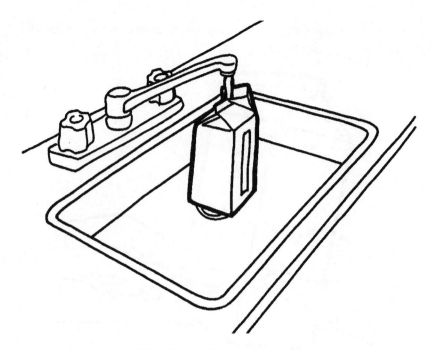

Fig. 11-3. *Fill the carton with water.*

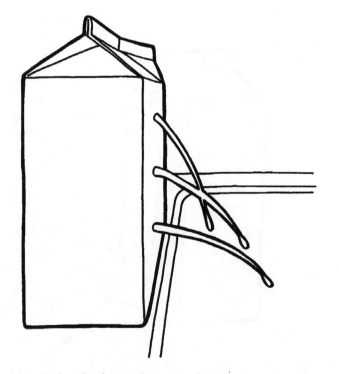

Fig. 11-4. *The deeper the water, the more pressure it has.*

12
Water Pressure and the Size of the Container

Materials

- MILK CARTON
- SMALL FROZEN JUICE OR POP CAN
- NAIL
- CELLOPHANE TAPE
- WATER
- KITCHEN SINK

With an adult watching, use the nail to punch a hole in the side of each container, one inch from the bottom, and cover each hole with tape (Fig. 12-1). Fill the smaller can with water and fill the larger container to the same level as the smaller can (Fig. 12-2). Place both containers at the edge of the sink with the holes facing the drain and remove the tapes. The streams of water will spurt out the same distance from their containers (Fig. 12-3). You can see that water pressure depends only on the depth of the water and not on the size or shape of the container.

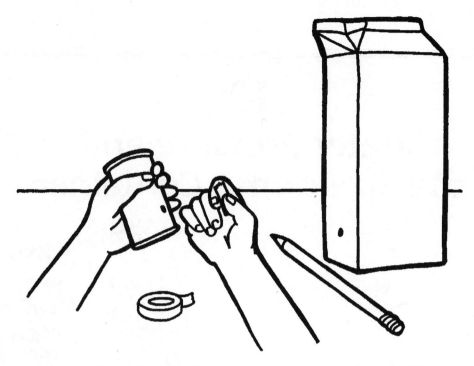

Fig. 12-1. *Make the holes in each container the same height.*

Fig. 12-2. *Fill both containers to the same height.*

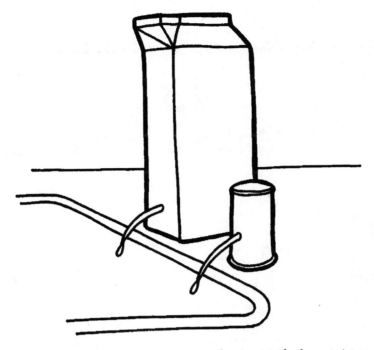

Fig. 12-3. *The water pressure is the same in both containers.*

13

How to Make a Water Level

Materials
- LENGTH OF GARDEN HOSE
- STRING
- FUNNEL
- WATER
- FENCE OR PORCH RAILING

Use the string to attach one end of the hose to a point on the fence (Fig. 13-1). The open end of the hose should be pointing straight up. Now lay the hose along the fence and bring the other end up to a point about the same height (Fig. 13-2). Use string to hold it in place. Use the funnel to completely fill the hose with water (Fig. 13-3).

Raise or lower one end of the hose until the water is flush with both openings. When this is done, a string stretched between the two ends will be level (Fig. 13-4). Pressure pushes on both ends of the hose equally, so the level of the water in each end will be the same.

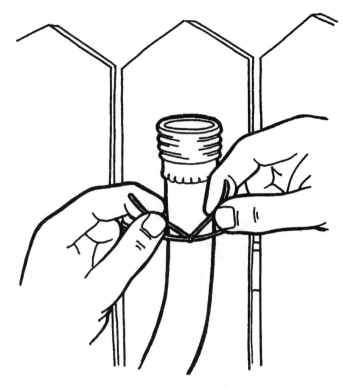

Fig. 13-1. *Fasten the hose to a point above the ground.*

Fig. 13-2. *Fasten the other end of the hose to a point about the same height.*

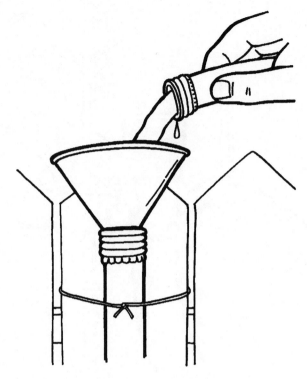

Fig. 13-3. *Fill the hose with water.*

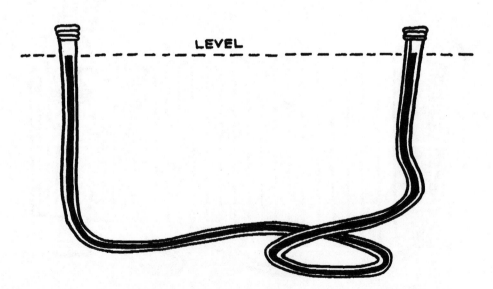

LEVEL

Fig. 13-4. *The water level in each end of the hose will be at the same height.*

14

How to Measure
Water Pressure

Materials

- CLEAR PLASTIC TUBING (ABOUT 5 FEET LONG)
- FUNNEL
- BUSTED BALLOON
- STRING
- CELLOPHANE TAPE
- WIRE (FROM COAT HANGER)

Materials

- FOOD COLORING
- WATER
- BUCKET
- FELT PEN

Have an adult cut a coat hanger for you. Be careful of sharp ends. Bend the wire into a stand to support an 18-inch length of tubing shaped into a U (Fig. 14-1). Fasten the tubing in place with tape. Fill this U-shaped tubing halfway up with colored water.

Now press the end of the funnel into the other end of the tubing. Cover the wide opening in the funnel with a layer of rubber from the balloon. Stretch the rubber *taut* and fasten it tightly in place with string (Fig. 14-2).

Now watch the level of the colored water as you place the funnel upside down in the bucket of water (Fig. 14-3). Notice the level when the funnel is just below the surface of the water, when it's halfway down, and then when it's near the bottom of the bucket. You will see that the colored water moves closer to the open end of the tubing as the funnel goes deeper into the water. This happens because water pressure increases as the water becomes deeper.

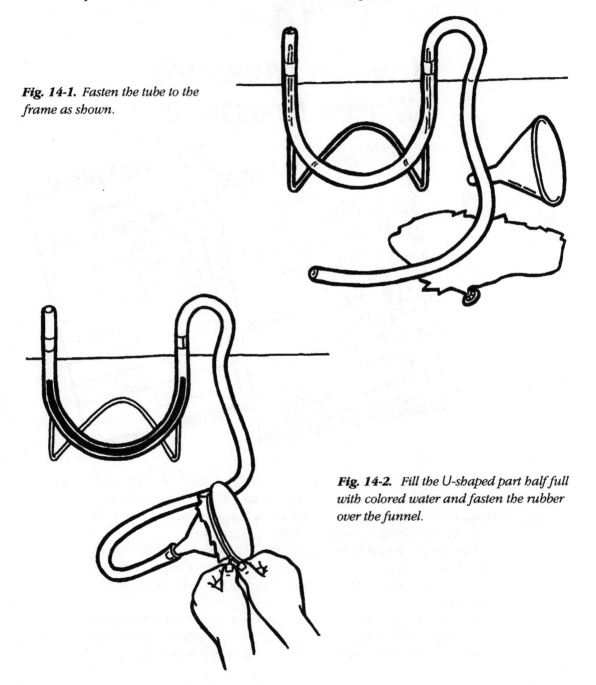

Fig. 14-1. *Fasten the tube to the frame as shown.*

Fig. 14-2. *Fill the U-shaped part half full with colored water and fasten the rubber over the funnel.*

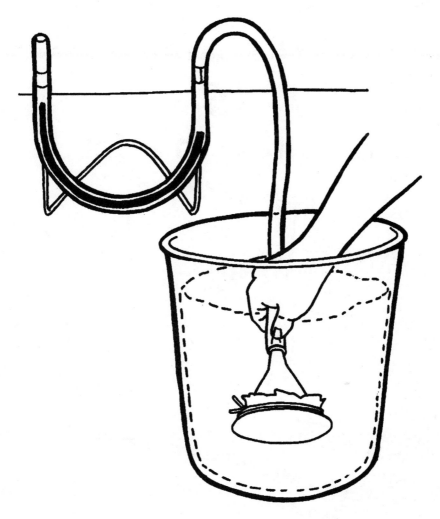

Fig. 14-3. *Water pressure in the bucket causes the colored water to move.*

15

Fountain in a Jar

Materials

- RULER
- SCISSORS
- KITCHEN SINK

Materials

- 2 JARS (ONE WITH SCREW TYPE LID)
- 2 PLASTIC DRINKING STRAWS
- MODELING CLAY
- WATER
- LARGE NAIL AND HAMMER

With the help of an adult, use the nail and hammer to punch two holes in the lid of the jar the size of the straws. Push the end of one of the straws about ½ inch through one of the holes and the other straw about 2·inches through the other hole (Fig. 15-1). Cut the second straw so that about 4 inches sticks above the lid. Use the clay to seal the openings around the straws. Now fill the jar about half full of water and screw the lid in place (Fig. 15-2). Fill the other jar with water and place it near the edge of the sink. Quickly turn the jar with the lid upside down and lower the shorter straw into the water in the other jar. You will see a fountain of water appear in the upper jar (Fig. 15-3). The fountain occurred because the water flowing from the longer straw reduced the air pressure inside the closed jar. The higher air pressure on the water in the open jar pushed the water up the short straw and created the fountain.

Fig. 15-1. *Push the straws through the holes in the lid.*

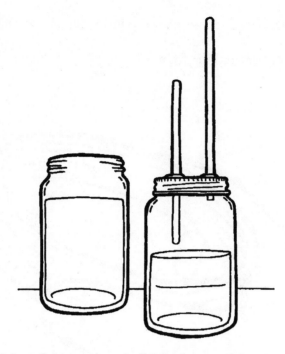

Fig. 15-2. *Fill the jar about half full of water and replace the lid.*

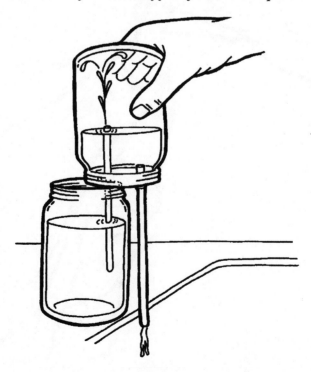

Fig. 15-3. *Water flowing from the straw causes a fountain to appear in the jar.*

16
Water and Friction

Materials

- 2 JARS THE SAME SIZE WITH LIDS
- A SHALLOW RAMP (BOARD WITH ONE END RAISED)
- WATER

Fill one of the jars about half full with water, and screw the lid on tight (Fig. 16-1). Place both jars at the top of the ramp and release them at the same time (Fig. 16-2). You will see that the jar with the water will start faster but the empty jar will roll farther when they reach the level area past the ramp. The jar with the water slowed down because of the friction between the water and the sides of the jar. The air in the empty jar produced no friction.

Fig. 16-1. *Fill one jar about half full of water.*

Fig. 16-2. *Water in the one jar will create friction.*

17
Why a Sprinkler Turns

Materials

- EMPTY POP CAN
- STRING
- RUNNING WATER
- HAMMER AND NAIL

With adult help, use the hammer and nail to punch four holes an equal distance around the can near the bottom (Fig. 17-1). As you remove the nail from each hole, push the nail to one side to aim the hole at an angle (Fig. 17-2). Aim all holes in the same direction. Now bend the tab at the top of the can straight up and tie one end of the string in the tab opening (Fig. 17-3). Place the can in the sink and fill it with water. Now lift the can by the string, and it will quickly begin to spin as water spurts from the holes (Fig. 17-4).

For every action, there is an equal and opposite reaction. In this case, the water spurts from the can at an angle, and because the can is suspended by a string, offering very little resistance, the force of the flowing water causes the can to rotate. Water shooting from a nozzle creates a similar force. If the nozzle is free to turn, as in a sprinkler, it will rotate.

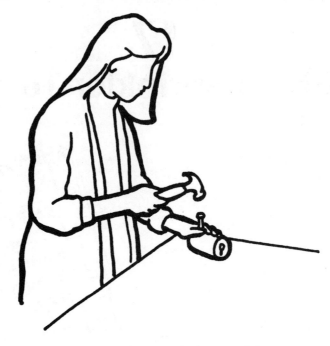

Fig. 17-1. *Punch holes near the bottom of the can.*

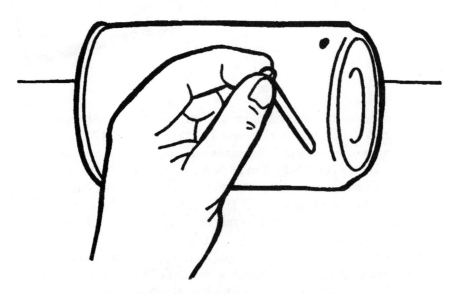

Fig. 17-2. *Bend the holes at an angle.*

Fig. 17-3. *Attach a string to the tab.*

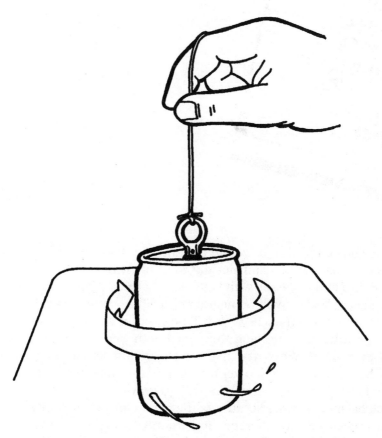

Fig. 17-4. *The flowing water forces the can to turn.*

18

Adding Weight to Water

Tie one end of the string through the nut (Fig. 18-1). Next, place the pencil on a flat surface and put the ruler halfway across the pencil (Fig. 18-2). Fill the glasses with water and balance them on the ruler. Balancing the glasses will be nearly impossible, but get as close to a balance as possible (Fig. 18-3). It will be easier if you place the glasses on the ruler, and, holding the pencil with one finger, adjust the pencil to balance. When you have one glass just about ready to go down, hold the string and lower the nut into the water without touching the glass (Fig. 18-4). The glass will go down.

The balance is upset because of the extra weight. The nut weighs less in water, and the difference in its normal weight and the lower weight is added to the water.

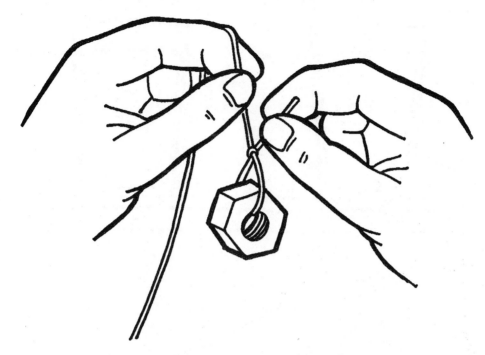

Fig. 18-1. *Tie a string to the weight.*

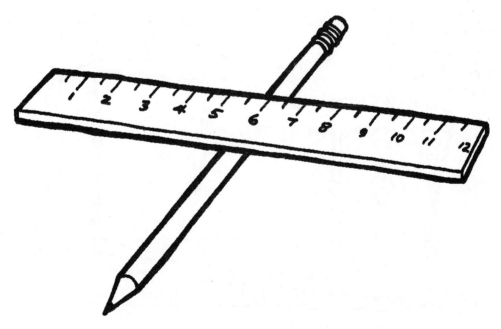

Fig. 18-2. *Place the ruler across the pencil.*

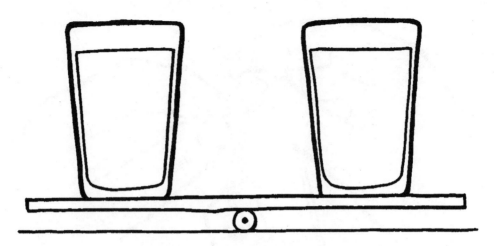

Fig. 18-3. *Try to balance the glasses.*

Fig. 18-4. *The extra weight causes the balance to tilt.*

19

How a Ramp Overcomes Force

Prop the ends of the yardstick and the ruler on the books to make two ramps. One ramp should be steeper than the other (Fig. 19-1). Loop three rubber bands together (Fig. 19-2) and use the tack to attach one end to the block (Fig. 19-3). Be careful not to poke yourself with the tack. Now lift the block straight up by the rubber bands and notice how far they stretch (Fig. 19-4). Next, drag the block up the steeper ramp and see how far the rubber bands stretch. Then try the longer ramp (Fig. 19-5). You can see that the rubber bands stretched the most when you lifted the block straight up. Then they stretched less and less as the ramps became longer and flatter. The ramp is called an *inclined plane* and can be thought of as a machine that reduces work. You use less force, but the block must travel farther.

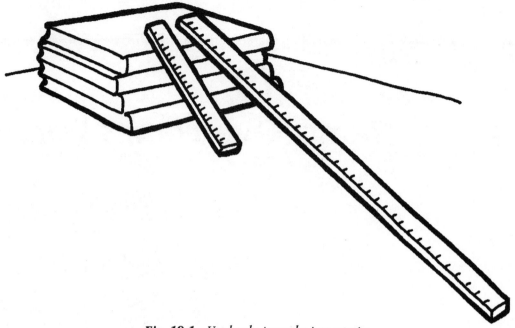

Fig. 19-1. Use books to make two ramps.

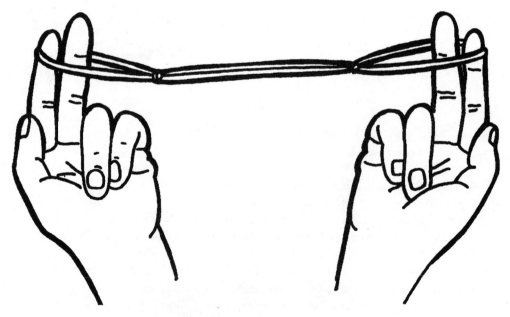

Fig. 19-2. Loop rubber bands together.

Fig. 19-3. *Fasten the rubber bands to the block of wood.*

Fig. 19-4. *Notice how far the rubber bands stretch.*

Fig. 19-5. *It takes less force to move the block up the longer ramp.*

20

The Screw and the Ramp

Examine the screw and notice how the threads are angled (Fig. 20-1). Now cut a triangle, or ramp, from the sheet of paper. Use the marker to mark along the cut edge, or the ramp (Fig. 20-2). Roll the paper onto the pencil from one short side of the triangle to the opposite point (Fig. 20-3). Keep the bottom, or baseline, of the triangle even as it rolls.

The colored edge, marking the ramp, will spiral up the pencil forming the pattern of a screw (Fig. 20-4). You can see that a screw is actually an inclined plane.

Fig. 20-1. Notice that the threads on the screw are angled.

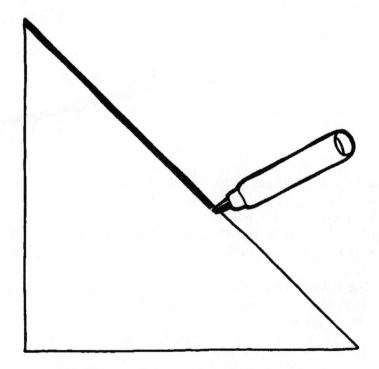

Fig. 20-2. Mark the ramp part of the triangle.

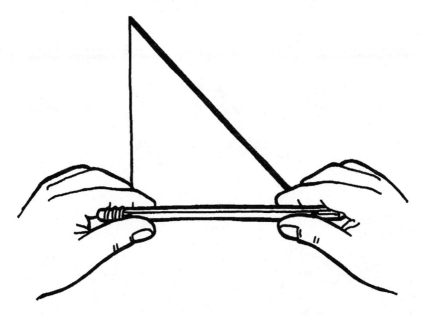

Fig. 20-3. *Roll the paper onto the pencil.*

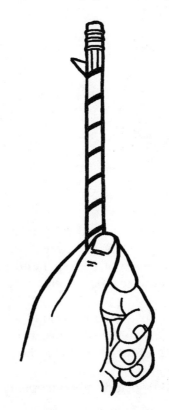

Fig. 20-4. *Angle the marked edge like the threads on the screw.*

21
Leverage

Materials

- HEAVY DESK OR TABLE
- 2 BOARDS ABOUT AS LONG AS THE TABLE IS HIGH

Place one of the boards on its end next to the table and the other board flat on top (Fig. 21-1). With one end of the board under the edge of the table, press down on the other end. You can lift the heavy table easily. The lever reduces the amount of work needed to lift the table.

The *lever* is a stiff bar that turns around a pivotal point called a *fulcrum*. The advantage is in the short distance between the load and the fulcrum and a long distance between the fulcrum and the point where the effort is applied.

Some common levers include a bottle opener, a seesaw, and a pry bar.

Fig. 21-1. *The lever reduces the amount of force needed to lift heavy objects.*

22
What Is Friction?

Materials

- BOARD
- PIECE OF SANDPAPER
- BLOCK OF WOOD
- RUBBER BAND
- TACKS

Tack the sandpaper to the board, being careful not to poke yourself (Fig. 22-1). Use a tack to attach the rubber band to the block of wood (Fig. 22-2). Now hold the rubber band and drag the block over the smooth part of the board (Fig. 22-3). Notice how far the rubber band stretches. Next, drag the block over the sandpaper (Fig. 22-4). You will see that now the rubber band stretches much farther. This extra stretching occurs because when one thing rubs against another, their surfaces resist this movement. This resistance is called *friction*. The rougher the surface and the greater the weight of the object being moved, the greater the friction.

Fig. 22-1. *Fasten the sandpaper to the board.*

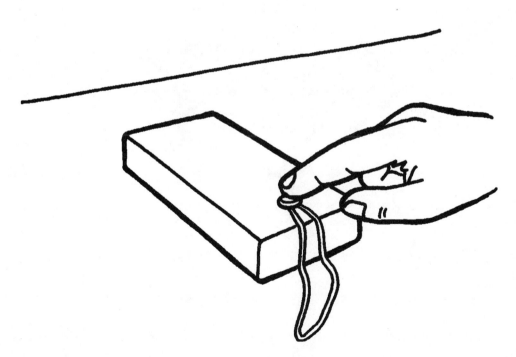

Fig. 22-2. *Fasten the rubber band to the block of wood.*

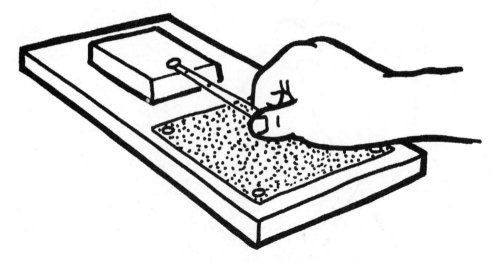

Fig. 22-3. *Notice how far the rubber band stretches to move the block.*

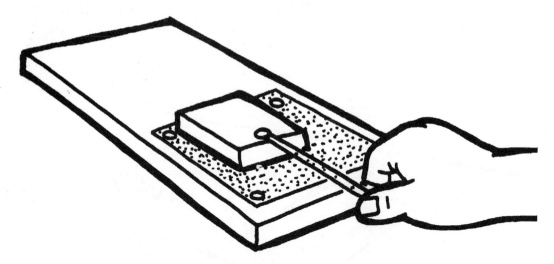

Fig. 22-4. *Rough surfaces create more friction.*

23
Oil and Friction

Press the blocks together hard and rub them together (Fig. 23-1). Notice how much effort it takes. Now rub soap over each of the surfaces (Fig. 23-2) and try it again (Fig. 23-3). This time you will find that they slide much easier. The soap filled in the rough places and made a smoother surface. The smoother surfaces created less resistance and produced less friction.

Friction creates heat, and soap dries out quickly. So oil and grease are some of the lubricants used to reduce friction in machines.

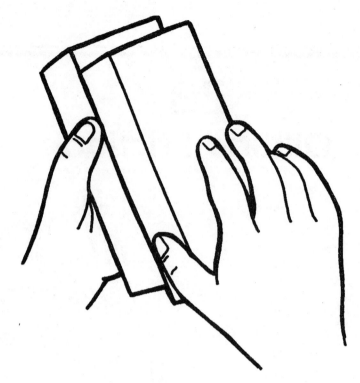

Fig. 23-1. *Rub the two blocks together.*

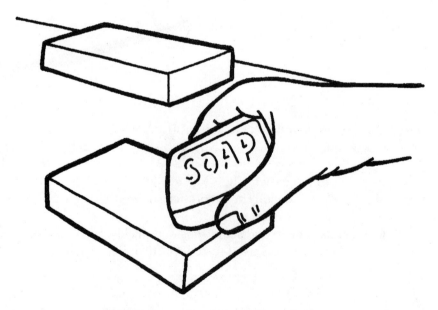

Fig. 23-2. *Apply soap to both surfaces.*

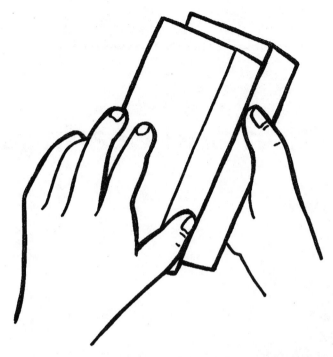

Fig. 23-3. *The soap smoothed the surfaces and reduced friction.*

24
Friction and Bearings

Materials

- MARBLES
- 2 TIN CANS THE SAME SIZE, WITH GROOVES AROUND THE TOP (PAINT CANS)

Find 2 cans with grooves that are the same size (Fig. 24-1). Place one can on top of the other and try to rotate the top can (Fig. 24-2). There is a lot of friction. Now place marbles in the groove in one of the cans (Fig. 24-3). Turn the other can upside down and place it on top of the marbles. The groove should fit over the marbles (Fig. 24-4). Now see how easy the top can rotates. The marbles act as ball bearings and reduce the friction. Ball bearings are hard and very little contact is made between the surfaces.

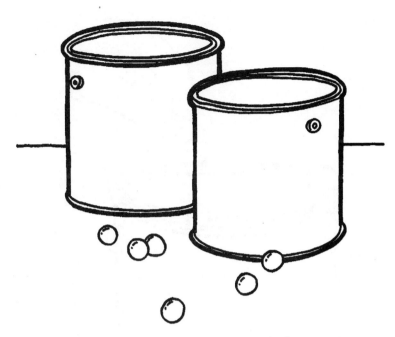

Fig. 24-1. *Use cans the same size with grooves.*

Fig. 24-2. *Try to turn the top can.*

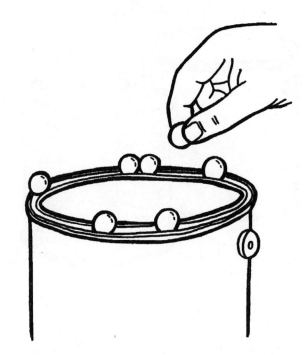

Fig. 24-3. *Place marbles in the grooves.*

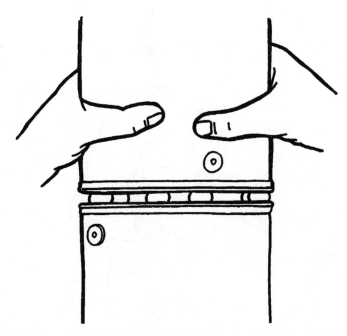

Fig. 24-4. *The marbles act as bearings and reduce friction.*

25

Static Friction
and Moving Friction

Materials

- SEVERAL RUBBER BANDS
- PENCIL
- SHOE BOX WITH SOMETHING INSIDE FOR WEIGHT
- SMOOTH FLOOR

Loop all of the rubber bands together (Fig. 25-1). Then punch a hole in one end of the box with a blunt pencil and thread the end of the rubber bands through the hole. Use the pencil to keep them from slipping back out (Fig. 25-2). Place some weight in the box (Fig. 25-3). Now hold the free end of the rubber bands and stretch them out until the box starts to move. Notice how far they stretched. When the box is moving, notice how far the rubber bands are stretched to keep the box moving (Fig. 25-4). You will see that the rubber bands are stretched farther to get the box moving than to keep it moving. This action means that it takes more force to start something moving than it does to keep it moving. *Static friction* is greater than moving friction.

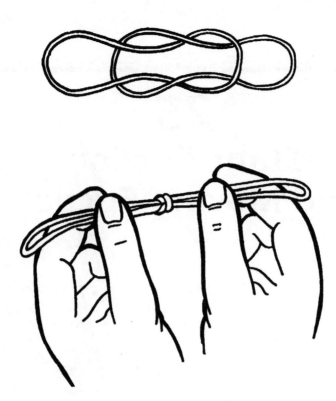

Fig. 25-1. *Loop the rubber bands together.*

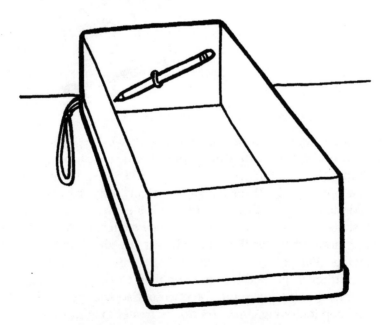

Fig. 25-2. *Fasten the rubber bands to the shoe box.*

Fig. 25-3. *Add weight to the box.*

Fig. 25-4. *It takes more force to start something moving than it does to keep it moving.*

26
Action and Reaction

Materials

- WOODEN BOARD (ABOUT 12 INCHES LONG)
- 3 LARGE NAILS
- HAMMER
- HEAVY RUBBER BAND
- 2 WOODEN SPOOLS (FROM SEWING THREAD)

Materials

- STRING
- SMALL POTATO
- MATCH

With the help of an adult, hammer the three nails a little way into the board (Fig. 26-1). Drive a nail near each corner in one end of the board. Drive the other nail in the middle near the other end of the board so that the nails form a V. Now cut the rubber band and tie each end to the two nails at one end of the board (Fig. 26-2). Stretch the rubber band back to a point near the other nail. Tie it with a short length of string and fasten the string to the nail (Fig. 26-3). Next, place the board on the spools so that the spools will act like wheels. Position the potato inside the rubber band near the back nail (Fig. 26-4). The potato must be small enough to pass easily between the two nails. Have an adult help you launch the potato by lighting the string with the match (Fig. 26-5). The string will burn through and release the stretched rubber band. The potato will go one way and the board will go the other. This demonstration shows that for every action there is an equal but opposite reaction.

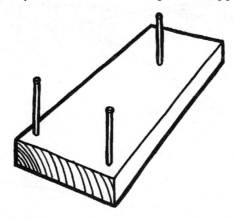

Fig. 26-1. *Drive three nails part way into the board.*

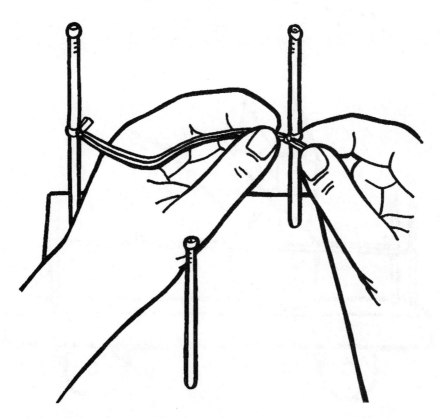

Fig. 26-2. *Fasten the rubber band to the two nails.*

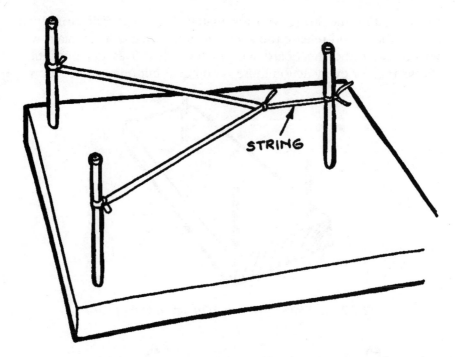

Fig. 26-3. *Stretch the rubber band back to the other nail.*

Fig. 26-4. *Place the potato in front of the stretched rubber band.*

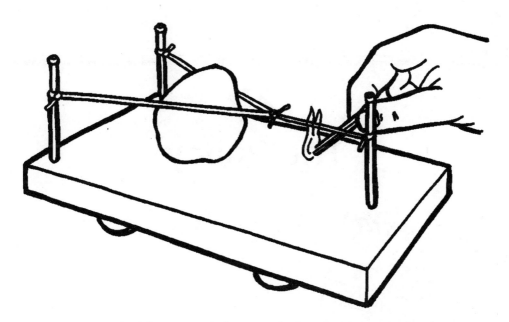

Fig. 26-5. *Launch the potato by burning the string.*

27
The Pulley

With an adult's help, cut a piece of wire, and thread one end through the spool (Fig. 27-1). Now bend the ends of the wire up with the pliers and loop them together (Fig. 27-2). Fasten the pulley to a support (Fig. 27-3) and feed one end of the string over the spool. Tie the weight to the other end of the string (Fig. 27-4) and pull down on the end over the spool (Fig. 27-5). With only one pulley, the downward force used to lift the weight is the same as the weight itself. The only advantage with one pulley is that you can pull from a different direction and add your weight to the force of the pull.

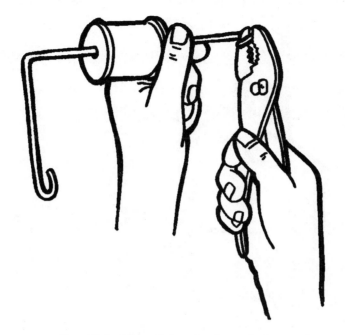

Fig. 27-1. *Thread the wire through the spool.*

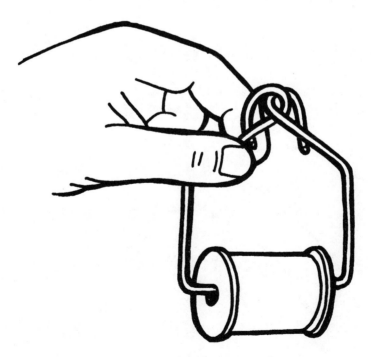

Fig. 27-2. *Bend the wire into a loop.*

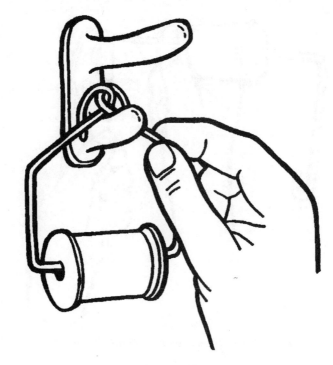

Fig. 27-3. *Attach the pulley to a support.*

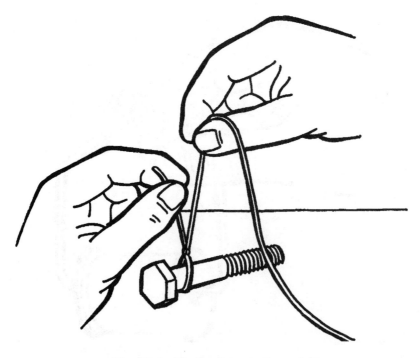

Fig. 27-4. *Tie the string to the weight.*

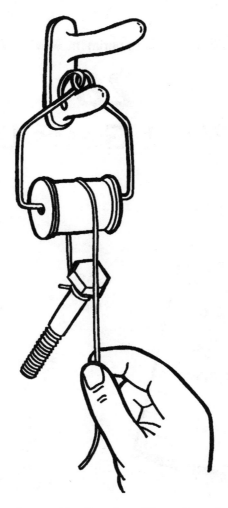

Fig. 27-5. *A pulley changes the direction of the pull used to lift the weight.*

28
What Gears Do

Find three bottle caps that haven't been bent. With an adult's help, fasten one to the board with a nail driven through the center of the cap. Don't hammer the nail too far because the cap must be free to turn. Now place another cap next to the first one and drive a nail through the center of this cap. It should be close enough so that when you turn one cap, it turns the other. Mount the third cap next to the second cap in a similar manner (Fig. 28-1).

Now turn one of the end caps with your finger, and you will see that the other caps turn, but in the opposite direction.

The points sticking out from the caps act like teeth on a gear. The teeth from one gear mesh with the teeth of another gear, so that when one gear turns, it turns the other. Gears are used to change the direction of a force. By using a small gear with a larger one, you also can change the force and speed of the turning gear.

Fig. 28-1. *Gears change the direction of a force.*

29

The Advantage
of a Shaft and a Crank

Materials

- CRANK-TYPE PENCIL SHARPENER
- STRING
- 2 OR 3 BOOKS

Tie one end of the string around the middle of the books and notice how much force it takes to lift the books (Fig. 29-1). Now remove the cover from the pencil sharpener and tie the free end of the string around the shaft (Fig. 29-2). Crank the handle of the pencil sharpener and wind the string around the shaft. Keep cranking until the books are lifted from the floor. You will see that it takes much less force to lift the books. This smaller amount of effort is because of the length of the arm of the crank on the pencil sharpener and the difference in size of the shaft.

Fig. 29-1. *Notice how much force it takes to lift the books.*

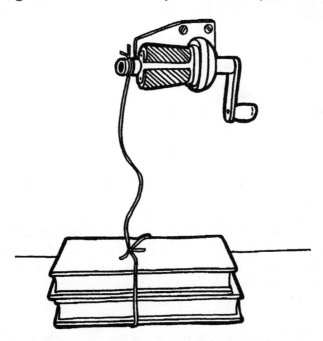

Fig. 29-2. *The length of the crank and the smallness of the shaft reduce the amount of force needed to lift the books.*

30
Inertia

Materials

- 3 COINS
- STRIP OF PAPER (ABOUT 2 INCHES WIDE AND 11 INCHES LONG)
- GLASS OF WATER
- RULER

Place one end of the strip of paper on the edge of the glass of water (Fig. 30-1). Balance the three coins on top of the paper and the rim of the glass (Fig. 30-2). Now, if you try to remove the paper slowly, the coins will fall (Fig. 30-3). Hold the free end of the paper level with the coins. Use the ruler to strike sharply downward across the paper about 2 inches from the coins (Fig. 30-4). You will jerk the paper from beneath the coins so quickly that the coins will remain balanced on the glass. The *law of inertia* states that any body at rest tries to stay at rest, while a body in motion will move in a straight line until it is affected by some outside force. It also takes a larger force to make a body at rest move abruptly than if it's done more gradually. In this case, the coins resisted the abrupt change and remained balanced on the glass.

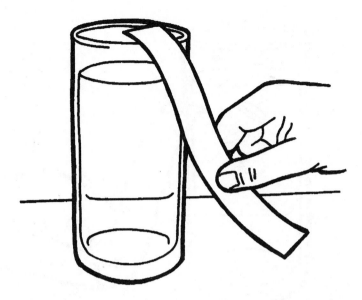

Fig. 30-1. *Place the end of the paper on the edge of the glass.*

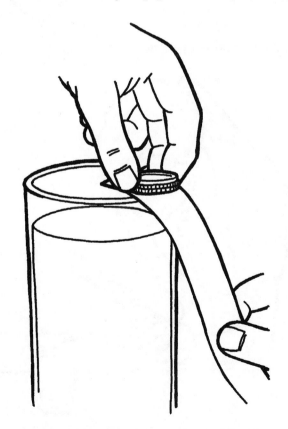

Fig. 30-2. *Balance the coins on top of the paper.*

Fig. 30-3. *Removing the paper slowly causes the coins to fall.*

Fig. 30-4. *Removing the paper abruptly allows the coins to remain.*

31

The Returning Can

With an adult's help, use the hammer and nail to punch two holes in each end of the coffee can (Fig. 31-1). Thread the end of each rubber band through each hole in the bottom of the can. Use toothpicks to keep the rubber bands from slipping back through the holes (Fig. 31-2). Thread the other ends of the rubber bands through the holes in the lid and fasten them in place with toothpicks (Fig. 31-3). Tie the rubber bands together with the string in the middle of the can and attach the weight at this point (Fig. 31-4). The rubber bands will form an X inside the can with the weight tied at the center. Replace the lid and roll the can on a smooth surface (Fig 34-5). It will travel a few feet, pause, and then return.

Rubber bands have a property called *elasticity*. This word means that the rubber bands can stretch and twist under a force, and when you remove the force, they will return almost to its original shape. Inside the can, the weight and gravity create the force that twists the rubber band. The twisted rubber band will store the energy you used to roll the can. When the can stops, this stored energy will cause the rubber bands to unwind and return the can to almost its original position.

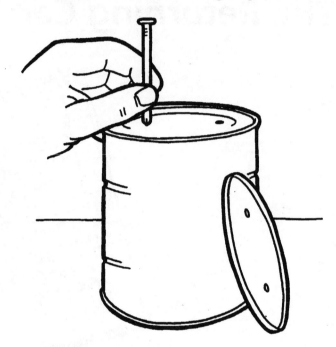

Fig. 31-1. *Punch holes in both ends of the can.*

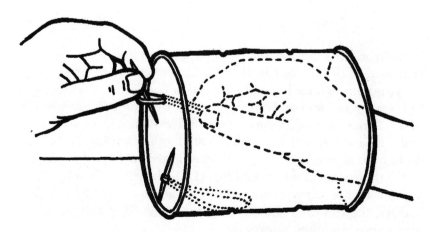

Fig. 31-2. *Fasten the rubber bands to the bottom of the can.*

Fig. 31-3. *Fasten the other ends of the rubber bands to the lid.*

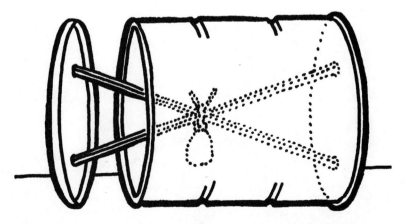

Fig. 31-4. *Tie the weight to the rubber bands and replace the lid.*

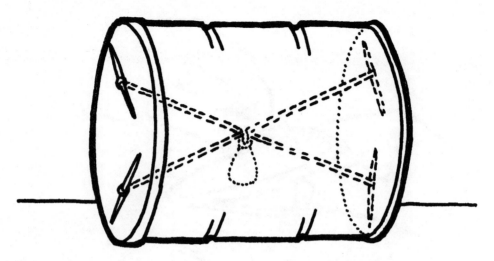

Fig. 31-5. *When the can rolls, the weight causes the rubber bands to twist and store energy.*

32
Simple Bridge

Place the books on a table to form two stacks a few inches apart (Fig. 32-1). Stack the strips of thin cardboard between the books to make a bridge (Fig. 32-2). Place the empty jar on the bridge to see if it will support the jar. It probably won't (Fig. 32-3). Now remove the strips of cardboard and place the strip of corrugated cardboard in their place (Fig. 32-4). See if it will support the jar. It should. Now add a few marbles to the jar (Fig. 32-5). Keep adding marbles to test the bridge. You will see that the single piece of corrugated cardboard supported much more weight than the four or five other strips of cardboard. Examine the corrugated cardboard from the side. Notice the tiny triangles between the top and bottom of the cardboard. These triangles form little braces that resist the bending forces. The regular cardboard did not have these braces.

Fig. 32-1. *Place the books into two stacks.*

Fig. 32-2. *Place the strips of cardboard between the books.*

Fig. 32-3. *The strips will not support much weight.*

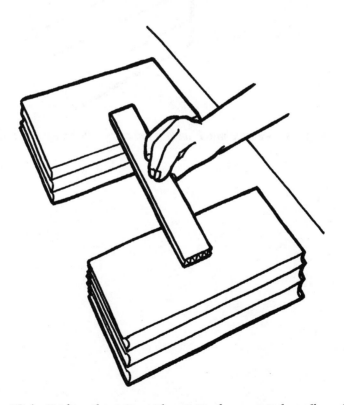

Fig. 32-4. *Replace the strips with a strip of corrugated cardboard.*

Fig. 32-5. *See how much weight the corrugated strip will hold.*

33
The Arch

Place the books in two stacks and lay the two strips of cardboard across them to form a bridge. Press down on the bridge with your finger and notice how weak it is (Fig. 33-1). Now remove one of the strips and curve it into an arch. Wedge the arch between the books and place the other strip of cardboard across the arch and between the books (Fig. 33-2). Now test the bridge for strength. Place the jar on the bridge and keep adding marbles to the jar (Fig. 33-3). You will see that the arch will support a larger amount of weight than a simple bridge.

Fig. 33-1. *Two strips of thin cardboard will not support much weight.*

Fig. 33-2. *Bend one strip into an arch.*

Fig. 33-3. *See how much weight the arch will support.*

34
How to Build a Truss

Hold the clothes hanger in both hands and notice how flexible the sides are (Fig. 34-1). Now cut the straw to fit the space between the bottom and top of the hanger (Fig. 34-2). Cut notches in the straw for a better fit (Fig. 34-3). Tape the straw securely in place (Fig. 34-4). Now push and pull on the clothes hanger. You will find it is much more rigid.

This design is a basic truss. A truss consists of an arrangement of triangles (Fig. 34-5). The triangles give the truss its strength.

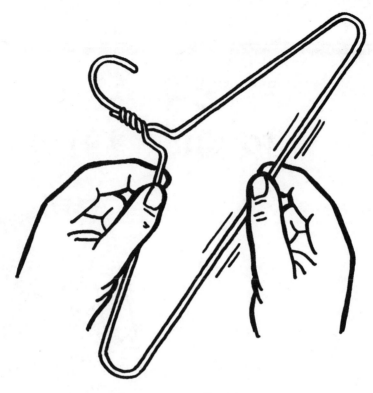

Fig. 34-1. *Notice how flexible the wire is.*

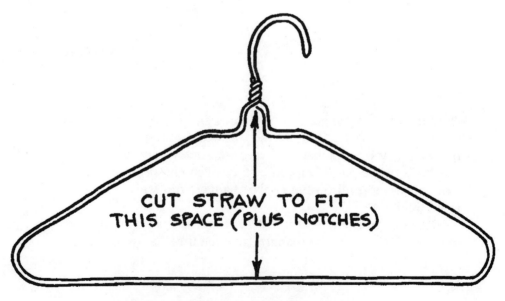

CUT STRAW TO FIT
THIS SPACE (PLUS NOTCHES)

Fig. 34-2. *Cut the straw to fit in the open space.*

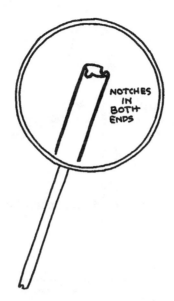

Fig. 34-3. *Notch the ends of the straw.*

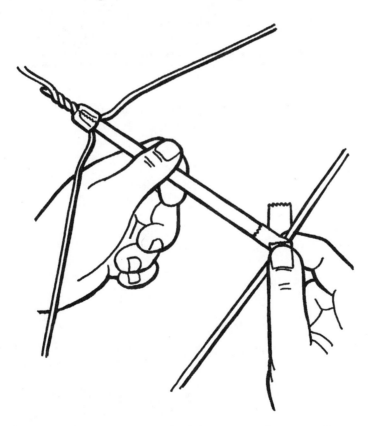

Fig. 34-4. *Fasten the ends of the straw to the wire with tape.*

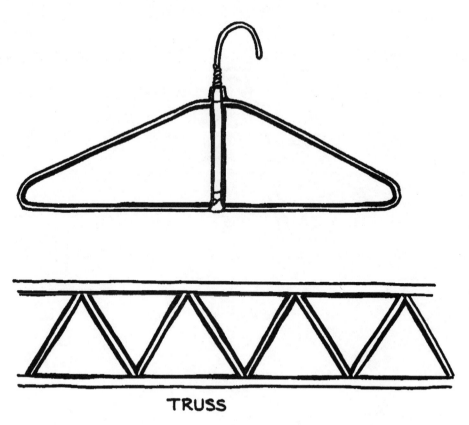

TRUSS

Fig. 34-5. *Now the wire will support more weight without bending.*

35
The I-Beam

Place the chairs back to back about two feet apart. Place the yardstick across the backs of the chairs like a bridge (Fig. 35-1). Tie one end of the string to the brick (Fig. 35-2) and suspend it from the yardstick (Fig. 35-3). Notice how far the yardstick bends. Now turn the yardstick on its edge (Fig. 35-4). You will see that it bends very little. A supporting member is much stronger if you place it on edge instead of flat. This experiment demonstrates the principle of the I-beam.

Fig. 35-1. *Place the yardstick across the backs of the chairs.*

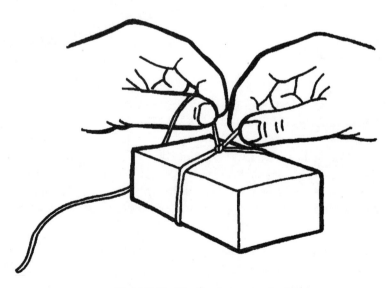

Fig. 35-2. *Tie the string to the brick.*

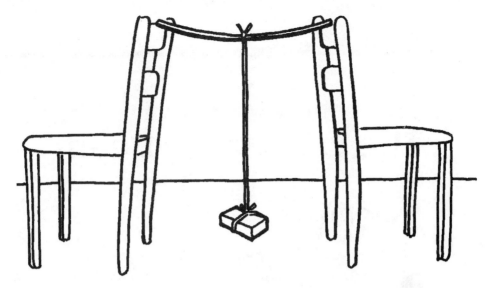

Fig. 35-3. *The yardstick bends under the weight.*

I - BEAM

Fig. 35-4. *When you turn the yardstick on edge, it will support more weight.*

36
The Laminated Beam

Place the chairs back to back about two feet apart. Put the yardsticks, one on top of the other, across the backs of the chairs. Suspend the brick from the yardsticks by the string. Notice how far they bend (Fig. 36-1). Now clamp the yardsticks together near each end (Fig. 36-2) and repeat the test. This time the yardsticks do not bend as far (Fig. 36-3). When something bends, one side is pushed together, or compressed, while the other side is being stretched. In the first test, the yardsticks were free to slide over each other. But when the clamps were used to keep them from slipping, the yardsticks became much more rigid. Laminated beams are made from gluing and nailing layers of boards together for added strength.

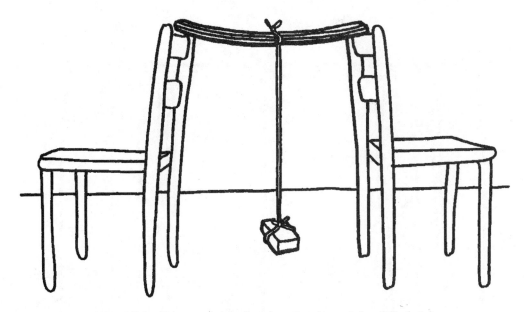

Fig. 36-1. *Two yardsticks bend under the weight of the brick.*

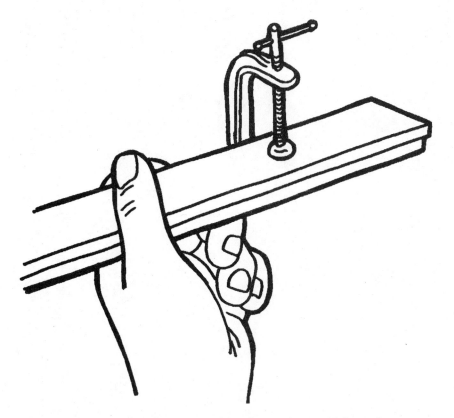

Fig. 36-2. *Clamp the yardsticks together near the ends.*

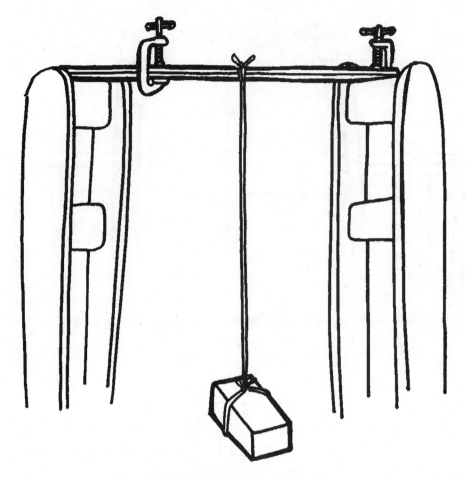

Fig. 36-3. *The clamped yardsticks act like a laminated beam and will support more weight.*

37
The Tube

Materials
• SHEET OF PAPER
• BOOK
• CELLOPHANE TAPE

Stand a sheet of paper on edge and try to support a book (Fig. 37-1). The paper bends and crumples under the weight of the book (Fig. 37-2). Now roll a new sheet of paper into a tube (Fig. 37-3) and tape the ends together (Fig. 37-4). Stand the paper tube on end and place the book on top (Fig. 37-5). It should support the weight of the book. When paper is in the shape of a tube, it is much stronger.

Fig. 37-1. *Try to support a book with a piece of paper.*

Fig. 37-2. *The book will fall and crumple the paper.*

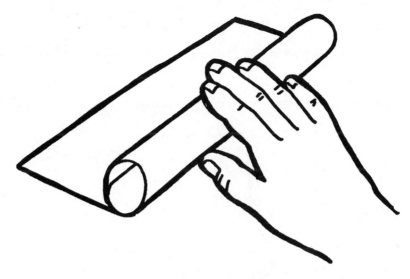

Fig. 37-3. *Roll a new sheet of paper into a tube.*

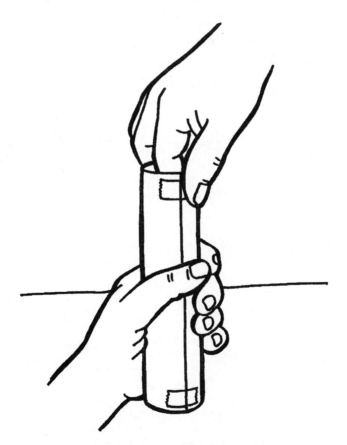

Fig. 37-4. *Fasten the tube together with tape.*

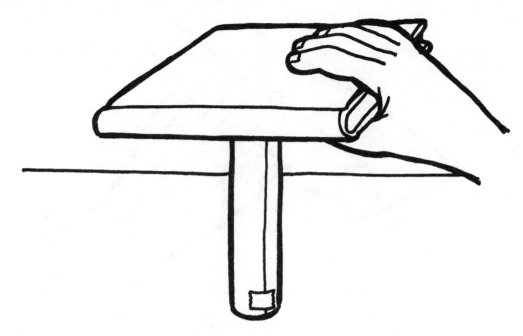

Fig. 37-5. *The paper tube easily will support the book.*

38

The Penetrating Straw

Hold the straw near one end and try to drive the other end into the potato (Fig. 38-1). You will find that the straw will penetrate the potato. The straw easily can be bent horizontally, but when used vertically, it is very strong. This idea works because it is in the shape of a tube.

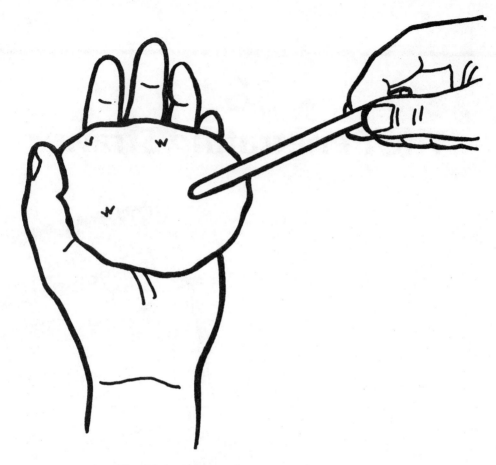

Fig. 38-1. *You can drive a straw into a potato.*

39
Strength of Domes

Materials

- 2 PAPER TOWELS OR A CLOTH
- 4 RAW EGGS
- SCISSORS
- SEVERAL BOOKS
- PENCIL
- SPOON

Mark a line around the center of each egg, dividing it in half (Fig. 39-1). Now carefully break one end of each egg by tapping it on a hard surface (Fig. 39-2). Just break the one end; you want to use the other end. Next, scoop out the eggs. Carefully use the scissors to trim the broken edges down to the pencil mark (Fig. 39-3). Try to make the edges smooth and even. You now should have four eggshell domes. Spread the paper towels out, one on top of the other, on a smooth, flat surface. Place the eggshell domes, open end down, on the paper towels. Position the domes in the shape of a square slightly smaller than the size of the books (Fig. 39-4). Now, gently stack the books, one at a time, on top of the domes (Fig. 39-5). The domes might be able to support fifteen or twenty pounds of books before they break. Domes are very strong because the weight pushing down is distributed down the curve of the dome compressing the material in the walls. This design causes the material to reinforce itself and gives it strength.

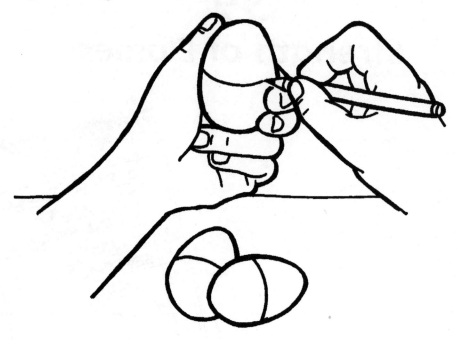

Fig. 39-1. *Mark the eggs in half.*

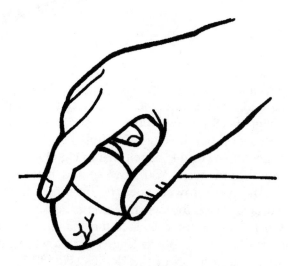

Fig. 39-2. *Break one side of the eggs.*

Fig. 39-3. *Use scissors to trim the edges smooth.*

Fig. 39-4. *Place a book on top of the eggshell domes.*

Fig. 39-5. *See how much weight the domes will support.*

40

Science Fair Projects

When someone looks at a popular science fair project, they often don't realize the amount of time that was spent on the planning part of the project. One of the most important parts of the planning stage simply is choosing the subject. A science fair project should be an exciting and educational experience, but if not well planned, it could be an exercise in frustration.

If you select a subject too quickly, you might discover later that the materials are not available or are too expensive or that the subject is just too complicated. In this case, you might abandon the project, and it might be too late to start another. Choose a subject you are interested in or would like to learn about. It might be something that you already are familiar with. Use your imagination, but try to keep your project within your abilities.

To begin your planning stage, you could divide your science fair project into a few basic steps such as: (1) choosing a subject, (2) questions and hypothesis, (the *hypothesis* is simply what you think the results of the experiment will be), (3) doing the experiment, and (4) the results and conclusions of the experiment.

Research is an important part of a science fair project. This research can include writing a research paper (Fig. 40-1). It will help you gather important information and narrow down your subject to a specific topic. You might want to write a report on your experiment. It should explain what you wanted to prove or a question you wanted to answer. Graphs and charts often are helpful in explaining experiments. Your report should describe your experiment, the results of your experiment, and the conclusions you made based on the results of your experiment.

When choosing a subject, think about the materials you will need. Often, you can find materials for experiments in items that usually are thrown away—items such as empty coffee cans, plastic or glass bottles, cardboard tubes from tissue or paper towels, and wooden spools from sewing thread. If your experiment needs a model, you probably can make it from cardboard or wood.

After you have selected your subject, narrow it down to a specific question you want to answer or a particular problem you want to solve. Don't generalize. Pick a specific point to prove. For example, if you were interested in wind resistance and airfoils, you might design a small sail that you could fit to a bicycle or a skateboard (Fig. 40-2). Or you could build a wind tunnel and demonstrate how an engineer designs an airplane for speed or for carrying heavy loads (Fig. 40-3).

If you want to show how gears are used to perform work, you could use an electric fan to drive a model windmill that uses gears from an old clock to do a variety of jobs (Fig. 40-4).

You could build a bridge from wooden matches to demonstrate the strength in a truss (Fig. 40-5). You also could build a dome to show an engineer's example of what buildings in the future might look like (Fig. 40-6). Use your imagination. Daydream a little, and you will be surprised by the number of ideas you will come up with.

Most experiments are displayed on some type of table or platform. You could set your experiment up in front of cardboard or wooden panels. You could divide the panels into three sections. Angle the two end sections forward slightly so that they will stand by themselves, like a theater stage (Fig 40-7). Use each section of the panel to display information about your experiment. The left section could show the purpose of your experiment, why you chose the experiment, and what you wanted to prove. The middle section of the panel might display a diagram of your experiment and why you built it the way you did or why you used the materials that you did. The right section of the panel can display the results of your experiment and your conclusions. This section also might include any possible future uses or applications of this information or any way it could benefit our environment.

You might begin with what appears as a simple experiment, but by doing your research and using your imagination, you could develop and expand this experiment into a very interesting project. A science fair should be educational, but there is no reason why you can't have fun while you discover something new. Sometimes when something is built for a particular purpose, it turns out to be more useful for something else. Accidental discoveries do happen, and engineers should be able to improvise. But generally, they design and build things that get the most use out of the materials available. Early man built rafts from logs and floated down rivers. Today we have the space shuttle. Most of the advances we've made are the results of some type of engineering. It is obvious that it will be a very important part of our future. Many new engineering feats are still waiting to be accomplished.

Fig. 40-1. A research paper helps you gather important information.

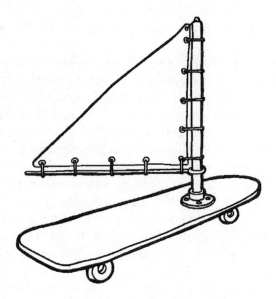

Fig. 40-2. *A sail attached to a skateboard could be the basis of an interesting project.*

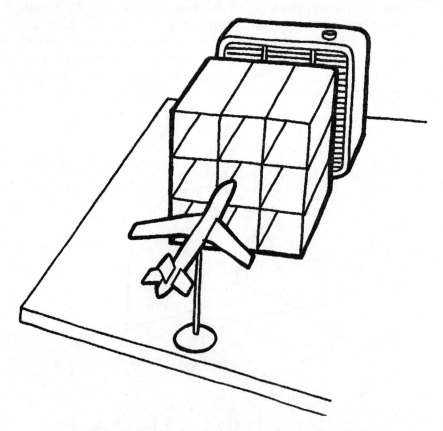

Fig. 40-3. *Wind tunnels help in designing airfoils.*

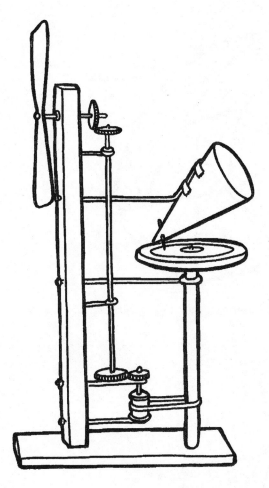

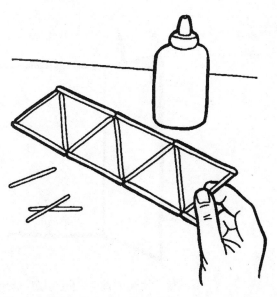

Fig. 40-4. You can use gears to do a variety of jobs.

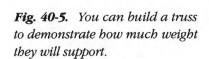

Fig. 40-5. You can build a truss to demonstrate how much weight they will support.

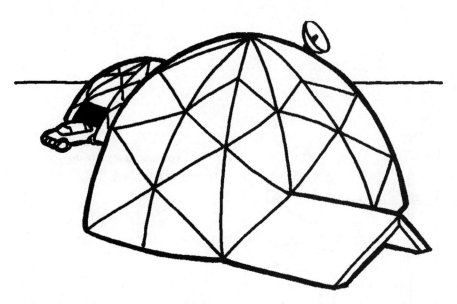

Fig. 40-6. *Homes in the future might be built in the shape of domes.*

Fig. 40-7. *A panel could provide the background for your project.*

Glossary

action   the doing of something; state of being in motion or working.

airfoil   a devise with a curved surface, such as a wing, designed to create lift.

aqueducts   a large pipe or conduit made for bringing water from a distant source.

arch   a curved structure that supports the weight of material over an open space, as in a bridge or doorway.

bridle   something that controls or restrains.

center of gravity   that point in a body or system around which weight is distributed evenly or balanced.

corrugated   to shape, or contract, into parallel grooves and ridges.

elasticity   qualify of being elastic.

energy   force of expression or utterance; strength or power efficiently exerted.

force   the cause that puts an object at rest into motion or alters the motion of a moving object.

friction   the resistance to motion of two moving objects or surfaces that touch.

fulcrum   the support, or point of support, on which a lever turns in raising or moving something.

hypothesis   a guess used by scientists to explain how or why something happens.

I-beam   a structural beam shaped like an I in a cross section.

inclined plane   a surface that leans or slants.

inertia   the tendency of something to remain at rest, if at rest, or if moving, to keep moving in the same direction unless affected by some outside force.

laminated   composed of or built in thin sheets or layers that have been bonded or pressed together, sometimes under heat.

lash to bind with a line.

law of inertia any body at rest tries to stay at rest, any body in motion moves in a straight line until affected by some outside force.

lever a device consisting of a bar turning about a fixed point; the fulcrum, using power to force applied at a second point to lift or sustain a weight at a third point.

pressure force exerted against an opposing body; thrust distributed over a surface.

reaction a return or opposing action, force, influence, etc.

stabilize to keep from changing or fluctuating.

taut pulled or drawn tight.

static not moving, at rest or inactive.

truss a rigid framework of beams, girders, struts, bars, etc. for supporting a roof or bridge.

wind tunnel a tunnel-like chamber through which air is forced, and which scale models of airplanes are tested to determine the effects of wind pressure.

Index